SAT Sneak Attack

How Computer Geniuses Hack, Beat and Cheat Americas Most Feared Exam

by Peter Wayner

HACKLEY PUBLIC LIBRARY
MUSKEGON, MICHIGAN

NOV 2 1 2014

Copyright 2014 Peter Wayner

All Rights Reserved. No part of this publication may be reproduced or transmitted in any form or by any means, electronic or mechanical, including photocopy, recording, or any information storage and retrieval system, without permission in writing from the copyright holder.

Thanks to Vadim Molochnikov for the cover image. (Flickr: molotalk)

Version March 17, 2014

Contents

A Party	5
College Board	9
Cheating Myself	13
Calculators	15
Blocking	17
Reprogramming	23
Business	27
Future	31
Biography	35

A Party

The kid laughed. Cheating on the SAT is easy, he told me. And then he rolled his eyes a bit. Didn't I know this?

The truth unfolded, as it often does, in a casual aside at the very end of a good party. In the fleeing moments when when everyone's guard was down. No one brags about cheating in a job interview. No one just brings it up on a first date. But this was one of those events held at a gorgeous mansion in the horse country of Maryland. The bar was close to empty. People were thinking about maybe, possibly, perhaps going home. If they could only get everyone in the car. Talking about the weather seemed lame.

One guy who came with me wanted a few more minutes to play some video game that he didn't own. Could I wait a minute? So I had a choice. I could stand around gazing at the pictures of the owner riding in a steeple chase. Or I could look at pictures of the owner hanging around with Michael Phelps. Or I could check out the owner rowing in the Head of the Charles. Or I could start talking with a young guy just out of college who was in the same boat. His girlfriend, a genius doctor-type at Hopkins I think, was deep in an argument.

He went to high school at Bronx High School of Science, one of the best public schools in New York City. They let in only the with the highest score on one very difficult exam, a test that many think is even more challenging than the SAT. He was probably a good match for a doctor at Hopkins Med School.

So I needed something to start the conversation. Did he know about the cheating scandal at Stuy, I asked. It was just in the papers.

Bronx is not alone at the top of New York high schools. Stuyvesant High is its elite rival in Manhattan that also chooses students with an insanely competitive exam. The very best and very brightest kids in New York City go to one of the two schools.

The newspapers were filled with the latest gossip about a cheating scandal that ripped apart Stuy, a scandal that was delicious and well-timed for the fall when seniors and their parents started to fret about college. A smart proctor noticed a student slip a forbidden cell phone into his pocket during the exam and started asking questions. When the talking was over, the school found a ring of more than 60 students who were snapping photos of the exam and debating the answers with text messages. All while the exam was in session. It had all of the elements that made a story irresistible: privileged kids, cheating and new technology.[1;2;3;4;5;6]

The guy at the party nodded and laughed a bit. Yeah, he told me, it was a pleasure to watch Stuy get nabbed. He loved the scandal just like everyone else.

What did he think about the punishment? Some were suspended but others were just allowed to take the exam again. Wasn't that a bit lenient? Wasn't the school going easy on their little princes and princesses?

Nah, he said. Cheating usually catches up with people. It all averages out, he said.

This was a bit of a surprise to me. I've taught college students at Cornell, Dartmouth and Georgetown. When I was hit by a cheating scandal in my class, I started taking an informal survey of other students and professors before sentencing. When I asked, hypothetically, for an appropriate punishment, the students were uniformly in favor of really cracking down. They wanted justice to be swift, harsh and very painful for the cheaters. It was always the professors who wanted to give someone another break.[7;8]

This guy was only a few years out of college. Why didn't he feel rooked by the kids at Stuy? Didn't he want them hung naked and upside down in front of the school for all to see? Didn't he want this to go down– cue ominous music– on their permanent record.

He started to get philosophical. The kids were only cheating themselves. The system was still working. Then he said that the courses didn't matter and so the grades weren't that important in the big scheme of life. When you put it in perspective, he said, who cares about some cheating?

Okay, I said. Perhaps there's some truth to that for the average pop quiz. But what about finals? What about exams that make a big difference in everyone's life like the SATs?

The SATs? He waved them aside. The SATs are easy to cheat on, he told me. Let's go back to Stuy. The kids at Stuy were cheating on something harder. They were cheating on a test at a school with whip-smart teachers, not the average schmoes proctoring the SAT. Anyone could cheat on the SATs. Forget about them, he told me. Let's talk about the way the kids were using their cell phones to cheat at Stuy. Now that shows some brains.

Wait, I insisted. Let's scroll back to the SATs. When I took the SATs they checked IDs and brought in special proctors. It was super-serious and my parents called it the most important exam in my life eighteen hundred times.

How was that possible? Did they implant special chips in their brains? Did they use lasers for signaling each other? Did they use technology?

He laughed at my innocence. I felt like I was the last person on earth to know. Then he told me how anyone could cheat on the SAT today.

College Board

The SAT is well known to almost everyone in America, except perhaps the kids who take its competitor, the ACT. Even the kids who don't want to go to college are often forced to take it by schools obsessed with the exam results. There's no reason to dig into the basics about how the exam is given or how the kids fill out the multiple choice answer sheets with the number 2 pencils. Everyone knows that.

What people often don't know is that the exam is written and graded in a well-guarded office complex in the woods near Princeton University. You won't see this place in the list of offices of the College Board, the non-profit coalition of universities created by the universities to help them collaborate on projects like building an admissions test that's fair to everyone. The website for the College Board (`collegeboard.org`) mentions only the main office in Manhattan and some branch offices around the country but it doesn't mention anything in New Jersey. This is because the test is produced by Educational Testing Service or ETS (`ets.org`), another non-profit that is also responsible for tests like the Advanced Placement exams. The two are technically separate but they are so closely connected that they seem like one organization to the high school student starting at the test paper.

The main offices of ETS are on a sideroad on the way out of Princeton. National Security Agency, the home of the code-making and code-breaking operations of the U.S. government, keeps a lab near by. It's a perfect place to keep the exams secret until their offered and make sure the results are tabulated fairly for everyone.

This locked-down fortress is part of the story. The College Board made a decision long ago to rely heavily on automation because it seemed like the only way to test so many kids at the same time. Everyone fills out the same forms and then the computers in this secret fortress make their inscrutable decisions.

The College Board invested heavily in this centralized technology because it offers consistency, an important foundation for treating every student fairly. The machines make the decisions, not the teachers who are only human and must struggle to avoid nurturing their pets.

But this model of centralizing all of the power in a hidden fort is far from perfect and it even encourages the kind of cheating that I learned about. The detached machinery in the fort may be fair, but it is also blind to much of what's going on in the exam rooms.

While researching this article, I've heard horror stories of tiny exam rooms, freezing exam rooms, and loud exam rooms. One school, I heard, just started demolition on the day of the exam and the kids were forced to soldier on as the room was filled with the noise from the jackhammers.

Students who complain about these poor conditions often discover that no good deed goes unpunished. There are other horror stories of the College Board's often heavy handed attempts at guaranteeing fairness. They can swoop in, cancel the scores for everyone in a room and force everyone to take the exam again, even those who did well. Hey you, their letters say, someone else screwed up and now we're going to ruin another of your Saturdays. Why? Because we can. And we want to be fair. Really, we do. There are plenty of cautionary tales who say that it can be better to keep your head down and not say anything.

The biggest complaints I heard were about the proctors. While I remember a serious set of people running the show, others did not need much prompting to tell me of proctors who didn't care about the test takers. It's easy to find stories about lazy or ineffective proctors who were barely able to stay awake.[8]

Then there are the cynical who told me of the mythical private schools who managed to only hire the beloved 80 year old former teacher who was now half-blind and almost entirely deaf. Perhaps she's out there, blithely filing her nails and ignoring the cheating of those nice-looking kids at her school.

A big part of the problem is greed. While many of these proctors are lucky to make a bit over minimum wage, the leadership of the College Board does very well. Fewer people know just how lucrative the SAT happens to be. The College Board, the organization that runs the exam, paid its last president $1.3 million. Tamar Lewin at the NY Times reported that they're clamping down on high pay now and the new guy is getting a base salary of $550,000. But that's just the beginning. When all of the checks are cashed, the new guy will probably pull in close to $750,000. It's a nice business.[9;10]

There's a reason why he's paid well. The money the College Board collects from administering exams is so good that it just keeps piling up. Rick Cohen writing for the Non-Profit Quarterly found the organization's tax forms reported revenue of $720.65 million between June 2010 and June 2011. Even after they paid all of their expenses that year, they still had more than $35 million left over. All of those checks written by the anxious parents sure add up.[11]

This is the big advantage of a centralized mechanism. The leadership can cut fat checks to themselves and every time they run out of money, they can bump up the cost of the exam a few bucks. A small rise spread over millions of test takers creates a big horde of cash.

Running a centralized business like this, though, requires keeping everyone else poor. The leaders of the College Board may get a fat salary, but not much of that three quarters of a billion dollars makes its way down to the people doing the work. It's easy to find reports on the Internet of people getting paid around $10 an hour to proctor the exam although it would probably be a bit higher in some cities.

Do they do a good job? I'm sure many do what they can but when the pay is that bad, it's no surprise that the proctors start napping or thinking about something else. In 2012, the New York Times reported that the College Board tossed out the results of 199 kids who took the exam on May 5th in Brooklyn. The proctors were "inattentive" and so all of them had to sit through the hell one more time.[12;13]

When I started finding stories like these, I realized my newfound friend at the party wasn't kidding about how easy it can be to slip something by the College Board.

Cheating Myself

Unless they invent a new entrance exam for the nursing homes, there are no more standardized tests in my future. I've made it through the meat grinder and lived to find a life and a career on the other end.

The exams never got in my way but I saw what they did to my friends who didn't get the corresponding scores. The ones who did wonderfully in high school but couldn't decode the SAT were doomed to live with going to a less prestigious college. Perhaps it wasn't a big deal in the large, panoramic picture of life, but at the time it seemed scandalous, tragic, and wrong.

Even now, after I've had decades to forget, I felt like this kid from Bronx was hurting my friends and, even worse, hurting my own kids who would be stuck taking the SAT soon. How could he be so cavalier about something that was corroding the future of my friends and my kids?

Was it really so easy to cheat? I had to try for myself.

So I plugged in a cable, went to the right spot on the Internet, downloaded some software, and pushed a button. Voilà. It took me a few minutes. I had to restart my computer once because I pushed the wrong button. But it wasn't too hard at all. I wouldn't ask a neophyte to do it, but I'm sure each school has several dozen students who are adept enough to do it. The nerds can stick it to the jocks by charging them some cash to do it for them.

The secret, my newfound friend at the party told me, is getting the right calculator. The average kid has a four function machine that can add, subtract, multiply and divide. The folks at the SAT allow everyone to bring in a calculator so the future leaders of tomorrow can be tested on more than basic arithmetic. The SAT is supposed to test insight and abstract thinking not the ability to add straight.

The trick, he explained, is that some fancy models from Texas Instruments can be reprogrammed. The average kids who bought an off-the-shelf calculator are stuck with something that will just add, subtract, multiply and divide. The rich kids who had parents who splurged on the best model from Texas Instruments have a machine that is just as programmable as a desktop. The trick was to buy one of these, he told me. The folks who proctored the SAT, he told me, couldn't tell the difference and they didn't care to try. When you're getting paid about $10 an hour, you're wondering if you'll be done in time to get to the early-bird special at the buffet.

Certainly reprogramming the calculator took skill, I pointed out to him. Didn't that mean that only the very smartest figured out a way to cheat?

Nah, he said. A few geniuses do the reprogramming. The rest of the world just downloads their work. I set out to find these geniuses.

Calculators

When Texas Instruments created their line of fancy calculators, they weren't aiming to help kids cheat– they just wanted to inspire the kids of the world to do more than just add and subtract. The TI-81, their first fancy machine introduced in 1990, looked like a regular palm-sized calculator with tiny buttons but it came with a big screen for graphs. Kids could type in equations and the calculator would draw the graphs for them without paper, rulers or pencils.

It's hard for anyone who didn't grow up in 1990 to recognize just how revolutionary the TI-81 was at the time. Back then, laptop machines were rare, desktop machines routinely cost thousands of dollars, and most college students needed to go to a special lab to use the school's computers. Most kids didn't own their own. In 1990, I watched someone pay $5000 for a Mac IIci and I thought he got a bargain.

The TI-81 came with a Zilog Z-80 chip inside, a big upgrade from the chips that were in earlier calculators. Even though this was a powerful chip that was the state of the art for desktops made just a few years earlier, Texas Instruments was able to use their manufacturing prowess to bring the price down to $110.[14]

This price was truly revolutionary because TI also offered the kids a chance to program the machine. Anyone who wanted to learn to write software for a computer didn't need to attend a college with the right labs or shell out thousands of dollars. They could pay $110 and slip the future in their pocket. At the time, the price was liberating and several generations of programmers wrote their first software with a TI calculator.

Christopher R. Mitchell, the author of *Programming the Ti-83 Plus/Ti-84 Plus*, told me that even today there are kids looking for challenges and the TI line of calculators is one of the best ways to learn the ropes.[15]

"The people who my book is aimed at are those who've never programmed before and already have a graphic calculator. That's true of most high school students in the US," he told me.

Today, Mitchell writes software for sophisticated networks of computers cooperating on solving the same problem. He works for companies using complicated algorithms to process huge collections of information. His work on the TI-83 taught him how to write simple software for a limited machine and his work is probably some of the most efficient. When you're creating software to plow through Big Data, the training from programming the TI-83 is some of the best you can get.

Other devoted Texas Instrument programmers tell stories of using the calculators and general purpose tools. Brandon Wilson, a programmer from Tennessee, said that he regularly uses his calculator to help debug and design other electronics.

"By the time I had gotten into it, a lot of people had written a lot of games." he told me. "I wasn't interested in games. I wanted to write real software. I would write a lot of utilities that would expand what the OS could do."

He writes code that others can use their calculator to probe the depths of other electronics like the Sony Playstation 3 or the average PC. With a bit of reconfiguration, a TI calculator can act like a USB drive and control the booting of a PC or a PS3, something essential for fixing bugs and solving deep problems.

"I have a friend who needed a keyboard in the work environment and he couldn't bring one in." said Wilson. "But he could bring in his calculator. It's convenient. You can bring it in to some tight spots. I use it as a diagnostic tool."

Not everyone has taken the same path. One grown-up software engineer who hacks the Texas Instrument line of calculators told me the same bright story of how the calculator introduced him to the power of controlling the machines.

"I started in 7th grade when I first started using a calculator," he told me. "I got the user manual and read it front to back."

Then he added something with a bit of foreboding, "It's always been fascinating to take a limited set of instructions and do things that they haven't even considered."

Blocking

The College Board and Texas Instruments have considered the way the calculators can be used for cheating. They're not blind or stupid. The College Board has a comprehensive policy on its web site and it forbids some of the most obvious ways that electronic devices can be used. When I contacted the College Board and asked for an interview to discuss some of the activities of these hackers, I had to send multiple requests. In the end, they just sent me another copy of the policy that's available on their web site and a few comments about how the calculators will still be allowed on the new version.

The basics of the policy are simple:

- No laptops.

- No mobile phones even if they have a calculator app on them.

- Nothing with a "pen-input" or "stylus-driven" interface.

- Nothing with a "QWERTY" or "keyboard-like" keypad.

- Nothing that uses an electrical outlet.

- Nothing that uses paper.

- Nothing that makes noise.

The list is fairly complete but they also include several catch-alls like a ban on "portable" or "handheld" computers. Despite the fact that the TI calculators have taught millions to program a computer, the College Board doesn't consider them "computers". They're merely "calculators". The College Board publishes an explicit list of acceptable "calculators" and the most common devices from TI are all there. There are also a number from Casio, Sharp and Hewlett-Packard. Many of these are also programmable in some sense, but the hackers I've interviewed focus on the TI.

The rules even seem to go out of the their way to push the fancier machines. After the calculator policy explains that anyone can solve all of the math problems on the SAT with pencil and paper, the policy explicitly discourages using basic four-function calculators. The best solution, it claims, is either a scientific or graphing calculator like the ones sold by TI. They explicitly say that either "programmable or nonprogrammable" calculators are permitted.

While the policy seems straight forward, any student reading it will start to find odd inconsistencies. After saying that anyone can solve the test without a calculator, the policy first discourages using a basic machine and then it says, "Don't buy an expensive, sophisticated calculator just to take the test. Although you can use them for the test, more sophisticated calculators are not required for any problem on the test." They also seem to backtrack on some of their absolute rules. The EL-9600 from Sharp, for instance, has a stylus, but you're just not allowed to use it during the test. It's not clear what they want the kids to do.

For its part, Texas Instruments has struggled with the cleverness of kids. On one hand, it wants to encourage the kind of technical prowess to use all of the power in calculators. On the other, it doesn't want to help the kids cheat.

"While new technology didnt create plagiarism or cheating, students will continue to have access to new tools that, if abused, can contribute to the problem." said a spokeswoman for Texas Instruments to me in a prepared statement. "TI firmly believes that technologys benefits for learning far outweigh the negative ways some students may choose to use these devices."

The company has also developed several innovative tools and mechanisms for helping the teachers corral the students. They operate an online forum so the teachers can discuss strategies and offer training courses that can help teachers spot "common signs indicating student misuse of a device."

They also distributed two programs called "TestGuard™"

and "Press-to-Test" that will clean out some of the extra information and applications that might be on a calculator. They are housekeeping applications that help the teachers destroy the tools that some kids use to cheat.

One of the hackers I interviewed said that Texas Instruments was very sensitive about its relationship with the College Board. TI wanted to encourage as much creative use of their calculators as they could but they didn't want to be banned from the exam.

This is probably why the TI calculators can only communicate with wires, the kind that would be very visible stretched between the desks of test takers. While most hand-held devices can easily connect with the Internet and each other, TI left this power out of their machines.

Some of the people experimenting with the TI machine don't want to enable this either. Christopher Mitchell told me "I wrote a networking protocol for the calculator and so far I've kept it to a wired protocol. I haven't really explored how to make it wireless so people would cheat in class or cheat during the SATs. That would be a problem."

One hacker also explained that the creators of the SAT wanted to stop copies of the exam from leaking out. They often want to reuse the questions, not just to save money but to try to measure the relative difficulty of the different versions. This is why there's a prohibition on any QWERTY keyboards that would make it easier to type in the questions.

The spokeswoman from Texas Instruments reiterated this point, telling me, "TI technology is built with certain design limitations, such as lack of internet access and non-QWERTY keyboard configuration, to meet standardized testing guidelines that minimize cheating potential in these environments."

The TI calculators do accept alphabetical input, though, but the user must type it using the calculator's odd arrangement of keys. This isn't an ironclad solution. One hacker who's spent a long time with the Texas Instrument machines admits that it's a limitation but thinks that he could easily type up a copy of the exam if he didn't worry about his score.

The SAT's competitor, the ACT, has a more stringent calculator policy that explicitly bans some so-called calculators that the College Board allows. The TI-89 and the TI-NSpire CAS, for instance, are two handhelds that violate the policy banning "calculators with built-in computer algebra systems." In other words, calculators that can do more of the work for you.

The ACT's rules also include the catch-all prohibition, "You may use only the mathematics functions of your calculator if your calculator has other functions (such as games) you may not use those functions."

The College Board's rules don't offer this limitation, something that allows some of the cleverest programmers to baldly claim that they're doing nothing wrong. They're just using the basic features of their machine. In any case, there is no easy way for the proctors to enforce this without watching over everyone's shoulder.

Maintaining these rules and administering them is difficult if not impossible. The ACT's rules offer the ominous warning that **"You are responsible** for knowing if your calculator is permitted. If testing staff find that you are using a prohibited calculator or are using a calculator on any test other than the Mathematics Test, you will be dismissed and your answer document will **not** be scored." I feel sorry for the proctor who must enforce some ambiguous rules by telling a kid– a stressed out kid on the most important day that will determine everything about the future– that a calculator just isn't allowed.

Some of the other exams are even more strident. The GMAT exam, which is used to select people for business school, has this policy:

> No testing aids are permitted during the test session or during breaks. Aids include but are not limited to beepers, pagers, pens, calculators, watch calculators, books, pamphlets, notes, blank sheets of paper, rulers, stereos or radios, telephones or cellular (mobile) phones, stopwatches, watch alarms (including those with flashing lights or alarm sounds), dictionaries, translators, thesauri, personal data assistants (PDAs), and any other electronic or photographic devices or potential aids of any kind. *Note: If you require wheelchair access or need to use an assistive or medical device, please follow the process to request a test accommodation.* (Emphasis theirs.)

In other words, not only are calculators and practically anything electronic banned, you'll need to get special permission to bring in a wheelchair, a diabetes pump or anything that might even seem electric.

Reprogramming

The problem for Texas Instruments and the College Board is that kids are clever. Rules are just rules and kids find holes in whatever rules you make.

As one hacker told me, the game was figuring out how to do something that no one had imagined– yet. One clever programmer built a Klingon translator for a TI calculator.[16] His parents may still be nagging him to do his homework and his English teacher may still be asking for that essay on Jane Austen, but those assignments are boring because they've been done before. No one else has ever done something as cool as teach their TI calculator to translate Klingon. That's almost like creating real versions of the Universal Translators from "Star Trek".[17;18]

There are tens of thousands of programs for the calculators on the Internet and most of them do something clever and non-controversial like translate Klingon. Most of the hackers who work on the Texas Instrument calculators aren't interested in cheating. That's simple. It's been done.

Brandon Wilson, a noted programmer of Texas Instrument calculators, explained, "I'm far more interested in the technical aspects of messing with graphing calculators than the possible ramificaitions of it. It's always been my opinion that while I do have some responsibility when releasing certain tools, it's ultimately not up to me how people use them."

But if someone was willing to put in the time to build something that may be useful on a trip to the planet Klingon, it's not surprising that more practical minds have tackled translating the SAT.

Texas Instruments has waged an almost futile war against the geniuses who want to do more with their machines. They tried setting limits in the circuitry and the customers found ways around them. They've tried sending out cease and desist orders but that's gotten them little traction. The geniuses just keep working.[19]

"So far they've been antagonistic to anyone trying to put custom operating systems on devices." one hacker told me before sort of shrugging his shoulders.

"If it's going to happen it's going to happen. The vast majority want them to remain mathematical devices. I think only a few hundred people have calculators with non-stock operating systems."

Perhaps, but I think that he's underestimating. One web site distributes the "SAT Operating System" that solves SAT problems and the little counter on the web site says that 2901 copies have been downloaded at this writing. That's just a lower bound because it's one of dozens that are offering the tool. Once the files are downloaded, kids can pass them around or load them on the machines of their friends. It's fair to say that there many thousands of copies of just this free version.

Many hackers try to discourage the talk about the cheating. They aren't so interested in cheating on the SATs and just want to have fun with the device. They like the challenge of figuring out how to evade the security.

One hacker explained with some pride how he slipped through TI's defenses.

"The boot has a routine and it doesn't have any bounds checking." he said referring to the way that the calculator is supposed to double check that you're typing in a number of the right size. Good software is like a thorough security guard who paws through every bag and stares at every ID.

Alas, writing good software is hard and some of the programmers who built the original Texas Instrument software forgot to check everything. Then a smart hacker found the one place where the calculator fails to check the number and they can slip in a long string of instructions instead of a short number. If the calculator doesn't check– and it seems like it doesn't in several places– the hacker can now insert their own instructions and the calculator will follow them.

"If you can find a routine that does that, you can copy your instructions." into the machine, one hacker said. " There are simple ones that allow you to write anywhere you want. There are some where you just write too much into a buffer and it overflows. Things like that."

One hacker defended this as mere experimentation and fun. "You could write an OS on a cheaper model and it would have all of this functionality of the enhanced model." he told me.

"There are some very demanding games like *Legend of Zelda*. It won't fit in the memory that TI gives you. To run it, you would need to create an OS version that would have far more memory ."

The Legend of Zelda, however, may be fun but the same technique can be used to defeat the SAT's relentless focus on obscure words. One hacker explained how he created a long list of important vocabulary words and their definitions. Any user could type in a word and the calculator would explain the meaning, something that's invaluable for the language part of the exam.

While you're not supposed to use your calculator during the verbal sections of the SAT, the proctors often don't notice. If they happen to be patrolling, some students say the trick is to write the verbal questions down on their scratch paper and then return to them during the math section that comes later.

The hacker responsible for this program refused to answer my questions. On the website that distributes the SAT vocabulary list, he did include the disclaimer, "This is for educational purposes only, please do not use for cheating." Okay, that will stop them.

Not all of the cheating even requires using the clever hacking and glitching that some programmers have discovered to include their own operating system.

"One of the applications I discovered was Notefolio." one hacker told me about a program that makes it easy to load large blocks of text on the calculator for notes.

"What I needed to do was find a huge list of vocabulary. Once I found them, I had to put them into one package. For this one, it was more about creating some files that people could easily put on to their calculator instead of programming." he said. One site that distributes his work says that thousands have downloaded it.

There are indeed numerous examples of how to misuse the calculator. One video on YouTube from someone named "John-TechLocke" posted a video called, "Cheat On Your Tests and

NOT GET CAUGHT."

He describes how to store information on the calculator so it survives even after the teacher asks you to erase the RAM. The calculator comes with an archiving function that he assumes that teachers won't know about. They can insist that the memory be cleared and you can comply without losing all of the formulas and notes you've stored.

At the end of the video explaining the technique, he announces triumphantly, "The only thing I have to do is unarchive it and I can read the information I stored. I can have an A in the class now."

The irony is that this doesn't help with the SAT because the College Board doesn't require that the memory be cleared. They explicitly say in their Calculator Policy that, "You are not required to clear the memory on your calculator."

Business

The world of reprogramming the TI calculators to use on the SAT is not just for furtive hackers testing their prowess. A company called "Calc-Tech" sells a version of the "SAT Operating System" filled with sophisticated routines for solving many of the most common math problems found on the SAT. They run a web site, collect money and operate what appears to be a very legit business in helping kids boost their SAT scores.

"This app **solves SAT math problems** for you DURING the test." says the company's web site. "It allows you to work problems faster and with greater accuracy than you ever could by hand or with a graphing calculator alone. Its use is permitted under The College Board's official Calculator Policy."

The company claims that over 17,000 students have purchased the product for $14.95 and that these customers were "able to improve their score on the SAT test by **over 60 points** (on average) just by using this software." (Their emphasis in both cases.)

Those are bold claims but they're understandable. The software doesn't just do arithmetic, it tries to solve the problem for you. One section announces, "This program allows you to calculate any unknown of a triangle given sufficient information." All you need to do is use an "x" for the unknown value and the software will work backwards to figure it out.

Prime numbers, for instance, are a popular topic for the mathematics sections. The SAT Operating System has one function that tests any number and tells you if it's prime. Is 51 prime? What about 89? It will tell you in the time it takes to punch in the digits.

The software is, in many respects, a good deal. There are dozens of formulas hard coded so the software is ready to handle most of the problems that the test will throw at you. It will find the lengths of the sides of right triangles and save you the trouble of remembering the Pythagorean theorem. It's easy to see why scores rise for those who let the calculator do the thinking.

The FAQ for the software explains, "All you have to do is type in your values and an answer is returned to you. You never have to worry about which equation to use. Simply select the feature that pertains to the current problem like 'triangles' or 'circles' and solve the problem without having to know a single equation."

Does this go too far? Steve Suchora, the founder of Calc-Tech, said in an interview, "The purpose of this software is to help students work problems faster and with greater accuracy. It is not to be used as a crutch. Our users still have to know the approach to a problem in order to succeed on the exam, but the software does help them save valuable time that can be used to work unsolved problems or to review answers."

Calc-Tech offers another defense on the use of their software on the SAT with this statement in the product manual:

> The key to solving problems on the SAT I Reasoning math subsection is identifying the approach. Once you know the strategy, the calculations are just peripheral. This is why the CollegeBoard permits and allows students to use calculators and software on their calculators; they are interested in whether or not you know how to approach the problems, not if you can memorize equations or make computations. If you want further confirmation, it is explicitly stated in the official SAT Calculator Policy that "you are not required to clear the memory on your calculator." In other words, you do NOT have to delete any applications, software, or programs on your calculator prior to taking the SAT I Reasoning math subsection; their use is permitted.[20]

This statement is fair– to a point. The software will not turn you into an Einstein. If you don't recognize the form of the question or the general area, you won't be able to get a reliable answer from your calculator. You need to recognize, for instance, that the question deals with triangles and so you need to push the button your calculator labeled "triangle".

The statement is also quite correct about the College Board's choice of policy. The College Board could easily take any number of steps to restrict specialized packages like this but they don't. They could ask the kids to erase their memory or just ban calculators like the TI-83 altogether. They don't and it's only fair for the kids who are smart enough or well-connected enough to invest in the technology that helps them get the best answer. If the rules allow calculators like the TI-83– and the list explicitly embraces these models– then companies like Calc-Tech are only working within the rules.

But even if the rules allow this, the software offers a significant advantage to those who can afford it. Using the software still takes much of the pressure off of the shoulders of those who use it. They don't need to work as quickly or manipulate numbers with as much agility. They can relax a bit, think more carefully and ponder their answers without worrying about running out of time. Speed is a big part of all exams and this software removes the issue for those who hold it.

Future

The College Board has just announced plans to redesign the SAT to be more relevant. The math section will focus on three areas said to "most contribute to readiness for college and career training." This will change the roles of calculators and eliminate them from one of the math sections but they'll still be permitted in the other. These changes will just reduce the power of a well-hacked calculator but it won't elminate them.

"Calculators are important mathematical tools, and to succeed after high school, students have to know how to use them effectively and appropriately." was what one nameless College Board PR rep told me in an email. "But the no-calculator section makes it easier to assess students fluency in math and understanding of math concepts. It also rewards well-learned technique and number-sense."

The changes don't really address the problem. It doesn't need to be so easy to cheat on the SAT. While the College Board has a difficult job administering a test across so many time zones, the hacking described here is easy to fix. The College Board and the calculator companies just need to sit down and solve it.

The simplest solution is to ban kids from using their own calculators. One company, discountmugs.com, sells promotional calculators that businesses can give away as advertisement. Orders of more than 5000 calculators cost only $1.34 a piece– with a logo. Blank versions are $0.96. These are solar-powered so there's little worry about battery life.

Providing calculators for everyone isn't a new solution. Consultants for the College Board have been making the same argument for decades.[21,22] The College Board could buy bulk copies in 100s of colors and distribute them with the test. Each testing site would get a random color so the proctors could tell if someone sneaked in a different version that just looked the same. (BTW, this is a potential loophole that seems theoretical but it doesn't mean that some aren't considering it. One hacker told me about how he was trying to insert wireless circuitry in his TI so people could communicate from calculator to calculator without wires. But it was "not to cheat", he emphasized.) Assigning random colors in sealed boxes would help block modified versions from slipping onto people's desk. The proctors would open up a sealed box on the day of the exam and discover the color used for that session.

This approach is already being used with some exams. The Graduate Record Exam or GRE required by many graduate schools doesn't allow any personal calculators. They hand out their own version with the exam and require everyone to use it. It comes with the basic four functions, a square root button and a memory for longer calculations. Everyone gets to keep theirs at the end of the exam like a prize buried in a cereal box.

Each section of the exam should also come with its own answer sheet. It's too easy to go back to previous sections to check work. Students routinely talk about making notes on their scratch paper and then going back to work on difficult problems. Each section could come with its own answer sheet and the proctors could collect them after that section.

The College Board could also start paying a bit more to proctor the exam. One hacker explained that catching someone cheating leads to a significant amount of paperwork and no one wanted to waste the rest of the afternoon filling out forms. The College Board might pay more to encourage the proctors to jump through the extra hoops, perhaps paying for the extra time associated with filling out the forms.

Technology is an endless cat and mouse game. It's easy to look at all of the gadgetry and give up. Just as that kid from the Bronx turned philosophical about cheating after he graduated from college, it's easy for the adults to imagine that it all works out in the end. That may be true for a long course with many homework assignments and numerous exams, but it's different for the SAT. One good morning with an amped up calculator loaded with all of the vocabulary words and equations can make a huge difference in someone's future. The College Board needs to recognize that there are tens of thousands of kids who are doing this, just an estimate from the numbers we can see on the Internet. The real numbers may be much larger. Fixing this hacking is something we can do now that will make the test fairer for everyone, even those without the fanciest calculators and the cleverest programmer friends.

Biography

Peter Wayner is the author of a number of books including *Future Ride, Disappearing Cryptography, Translucent Databases* and *Attention Must Be Paid, But For $800?*. More information is available at his website, `www.wayner.org` and through his Twitter feed `@peterwayner`. He can be contacted through the site. Please send any suggestions, questions, comments or complaints.

Bibliography

[1] A. Barnard and E. P. Newcomer, "At stuyvesant, allegations of widespread cheating," *New York Times*, p. A23, June 26 2012.

[2] M. Santora, "Amid inquiry into cheating, stuyvesant principal will retire," *New York Times*, p. A13, August 3 2012.

[3] A. Baker, "At stuyvesant, allegations of widespread cheating," *New York Times*, p. A23, August 3 2013.

[4] V. Yee, "Stuyvesant students describe the how and the why of cheating," *New York Times*, p. A1, September 25 2012.

[5] N. J. Girarldi, E. Bilofsky, J. Markowitz, and S. Shapiro, "Cheating at stuyvesant, and in life," *New York Times*, p. A34, September 26 2012.

[6] A. Baker, "At top school, cheating voids 70 pupils tests," *New York Times*, p. A1, July 9 2012.

[7] R. R. Ruiz, "Students react to SAT cheating scandal," *New York Times*, October 12 2011.

[8] M. Averbuch, T. Niu, and O. Fountain, "Pressure and lack of repercussions are cited in SAT cheating," *WNYC*, October 12 2011.

[9] T. Lewin, "Backer of common core school curriculum is chosen to lead college board," *New York Times*, May 16 2012.

[10] unsigned, "Backer of common core school curriculum is chosen to lead college board," *New York Times*, May 21 2012.

[11] R. Cohen, "Is the college board a nino (nonprofit in name only)?," *Non-profit Quarterly*, October 16 2012.

[12] T. Caldwell, "Sat service cites lapses in invalidating scores," *New York Times*, p. A16, May 18 2012.

[13] unsigned, "Sat scores invalidated because proctors were inattentive, report finds," *New York Times*, p. Choice Blog, May 21 2012.

[14] M. Martin, "Calculator museum," *Mr. Martin's Web Site*, – 2013.

[15] C. Mitchell, *Programming the TI-83 Plus/TI-84 Plus*. Running Series, Manning Publications Company, 2012.

[16] N. D, *nIQeyIIS 89 Klingon Translator*. ticalc.org, August 17 2003.

[17] G. L. Coon, "Matamorphosis," *Star Trek*, vol. Season 2, November 10 1967.

[18] M. M. Snodgrass, "The ensigns of command," *Star Trek: The Next Generation*, vol. Season 3, October 2 1989.

[19] D. Kushner, "For texas instruments, calculator hackers don't add up. after hobbyist cracks key to operating system, ti says: Cease and desist!," *IEEE Spectrum*, October 28 2009.

[20] unsigned, *The SAT Operating System Version 1.0- Operating Manual*. Calc-Tech, 2011.

[21] M. Protter, "Calculators are a wrong answer for S.A.T.'s," *New York Times*, December 8 1990.

[22] J. . Lee, "Calculators throw teachers a new curve," *New York Times*, September 2 1999.

Made in the USA
Charleston, SC
24 June 2014